My Courtship Into Loving You

My Courtship Into Loving You

One Hundred Poems and Then I Asked

Riley Hoagland

Title: *My Courtship Into Loving You*
Author: Riley Hoagland

Published by Riley Invents, LLC
Printed in the United States of America

First edition

ISBN: 979-8-9941199-1-4

Cover design by Riley Hoagland and Katrina Rupp
Author photo and Interior design by Riley Hoagland
Artwork by Riley Hoagland

This collection was written between August 13, 2025 and November 29, 2025.

For Katrina

Author's note: These poems were written in real time and most were shared shortly after they were completed. It was the way that felt most honest as thoughts and feelings moved through me.
Within them, I speak about trust, longing, tenderness, connection and more.

I appreciate you taking the time to read them. I hope you find the many healthy ways love can be felt and lived in your own life.

Brought from the sands
You bring me back to a full man
Resisting to reflect
Bracing soul for impact

Longing for
Longing in
Longing for
Longing in

Can it be once more

Sway with me
That milky way
Liquid thunder
Water works
Giving up, for what it's worth

Inspired
No longer tired
Be still
Stuck here trying

Appreciate
The ways
Shape of your face
Fingers full of grace

Swept up to be swept out
Letting go to be without
Going forward with a heavy lean
Makes more sense to stay between

Wooden lions of the sea
Dancing on sedges for you and me
The ways they wait so perfectly
Standing by so patiently

Waves and play
You make my day

Looking to see
If you and me
Can have a little time together

It isn't the time
For wine and dine
But rather conversation

It's me and you
So much is new
Grateful for this connection

There is little time
With kids and chores
Important not to be distracted

So silly poems
To uplift the mood
Can keep things moving forward

My heart lifts in my chest
With the thoughts of what's left

To touch and to see
What's allowed for me
Beyond and beneath
Trees sway as they breathe

Passion that's been felt
Closeness, and we swell
Surprises we find
Patience in the mind

Awakened by rain
We feel, just the same
Moved by earth
These whispers that are heard

Chest on chest
Until there's no space left
Press to pressed
You know what's coming next

Slowed eyes and deeper breaths
A hand reaches up for your beautiful neck
Tilting your face so my lips find rest
Where bone and gold, mark an "x"

Swirls of curls
Slowed down worlds
Lips to skin
Beats begin

So many places to take a rest
Let go of reality, to see what's left
Lives and lines and curves that flow
Ideas and thoughts, so much to grow

Beauty and wonder exposed are quite a delight
Try as I might, this image is alive
To dim the lights and kiss long lines
Two hours too lucky, for a late night drive

Simple is insufficient to say what I see
Vulnerability and courage are what speak to me
Taking this in further compounds your beauty
No pinches needed, this isn't make-believe

Your waist
Your hips
The edge of your cheeks

Where we find ourselves sometimes
Doesn't make sense, I've lost track of time
Good morning darling, what day makes this
Good morning darling, another day we exist

Pushing past what feels like life
Accepting something that feels so right
Asking the past, is it different this time
Nothing is the same, so why ask why

Give tears a little dam
Quiet exterior
Full spectrum man

Back and forth the mind goes round
The sights, smells, the softest sounds
Like whooshing waves and harbor seal smiles
Think we'll stay, silently for a while

Where does the energy go
Think it's been lost
Seems so, what do I know

With beauty and belief
Again, "we will see"
Let go of that which is
Gonna take another chance at this

Trickle and flow
This is the way to go
A meandering path, stumps and sticks
Pick it up now since again we exist

It became clear, like breezes thru my hair
The reasons of love existing here
Where sand meets surf, the edge of my world
Seasons and sandwiches, sea misted curls

Struggle to stay, some chapters are that way
Used as grounds to exist, release and play
Many makers met, lives changed, sit and pray
Finding yourself, meteors and sunsets, the longest days

Wear me down, let me stand at the edge
Lovers met and lovers left
Show me the energy never spent
No grass on the other side of this watery fence

Tipping thru
Slipping in
Catching silvers
Trust begins

Little efforts
Slowed
Letting go
Slowed

Temper
Trust
We aren't giving up

Thread
Connect
There's lots in our head

Pieces
Puzzled
Love gets muffled

Shards
Apart
Connections in art

Wait
Space

Say
Ways

It is going into
Another day

Hold you like a sweet stringed piece
Run my bow across your strings
Feel your curves round the place
Beautiful neck and smiling face

I wanna play you today
I wanna hear your say
Held me close
Keep me safe, play my strings

Keep me close
Play my strings
Let me hear you sing
Play me

Anytime that we are close
I want you to know
That I feel quite alive
Making music in time

Play my strings
Here's my bow
I'm trusting you
You know where to go

Give me peace
Protection
I'll give you back
...something goes

Speechless, seeing you in my weeds
Seeing how different it feels to me
Morning with goodnesses
I'm living proof, this is it

Blankets with shades of greens
Golden globes of life, you see
Piles of pullings, stepped over for me
Sharing in beauty, we believe

Caught in a moment with sun's kisses
Slowly trusting, shaking, what this is
Believing now for what is seen
Feeling more and more of the in-between

Broken
Busted
Not giving up

Glowing
Growing
It's not easy stuff

Hoping
Folding
Doubts turning to dust

Squeezing
Feeling
All this into safe love

Seeking
Being
Healing is rough

Keeping
Pleasing
Enough is enough

Living
Loving
Say yes just because

Trusting
Cussing
It's all so much

Distant clouds like kisses we've yet to make
Tinted like lips that meet your sweet face
Deep waters so calm they are yet to be known
Growing life and love so many call home

Taking slow breaths to begin our steep
Quality and pressure such threads we weave
Fabrics together in space, life and in time
Untouchable but tangible connecting our lives

Where did we come from so long long ago
What brought us to the places not yet known
Realities really matter as we merge to exist
Feelings fleeing returning to be trusted like this

Sharings saved and kept in a soft place
Grateful for opportunities to kiss your face
Lemme go get my all and have it ready
Getting closer, the foundation seems steady

For so long my toes have crept in sinking holes
Too many times I let myself find, "where does this go"
Not seeking sifting sands, wanting trusted land
Tracing and saving imprints, skin of safe hands

I'm awake, I lay. Transition over we play
What was it, 24 and some hours of the day
Steps to the truth, memories not to lose
Saving, playing, free to be, strength to choose

From the tops of the blossoms
To the tips of the wishes
Tap our chakras
Tune in to listen

Third eye wiring
Connected inside of me
Heart space
Finds a place

What's this feeling that seems so deep
The comfort
Friendliness
Being at ease

Connection seeking threads
Beginnings and ends
Sight with closed eyes
We take a look inside

Buzzwords and worries
Float inside the mix
Lucky are we
With fingers like this

Sacred messages sent thru space
Asking deep questions has its place
No matter the mind, history or time
Connection thru truth always just fine

Given the history and ways things have gone
Discoveries made and non-arguments won
To tell of a place familiar yet far
Goes with the rhythms, since we are stars

Heated we'll see where the mind is truly at
Step up, save courage, ready at last
Beatings and pokes of this mortal heart
Give attempts at making love with art

So give us this day, yet again awake
So much time has passed, grateful to wait
To give in to something, feeling so true
Giving love some space to feel with you

Lay me, lay me, lay me down
In your sweetest space
Take me, take me, take me down
To your centered place

Let this distance
Steep our time
Where you and I
Can intertwine

Strength to say
hold me, hold me, hold me
Where fears find holes
There's courage to let it go

So shimmer in me your golden threads
Your sounds resonate thru the bones of my head
Making memories not pretend
Walking forward, past where the sidewalk ends

Heavenly pebbles pulled and stretched
Heated and hammered to see what's left
Purring as we play with these golden threads
Connections kept quiet, the sounds of our heads

Flashes so clear, events with you
Seeping into all actions that we do
For just underneath such wild hair
I see you, your gaze, your lovely stare

Sweetness, slowly, bring me your lips
Gently, surely, draw you in as we kiss
This feeling, your fragrance, it's with time that I miss
Holding, heartfelt, human energies in bliss

Seven long days since your last touch
Spent lots of time feeling this much
Wonderful beginnings in seeing what this does
Sending photos and miss yous, just because

Seven nights through distance we slept
Each night in our nests, counting threads we've kept
Memories of sand dunes, lava rocks and waves swept
No longer needing to worry about dishes, no mess

From a long week, to many days, we have hours away
Racing with the sun to plant smiles with our face
Where we'll end up, we know it'll be a magical place
Hairs and threads, kisses and embrace, so much to say

Building out a place we see a foundation
So fun, to see it built with interest and intention
Bricks of trust, sand, heart, earth and love
Find our minds, with little left, come closer, hugs

Nests awake a primal sense
Capturing our primal scents
Giving in to give what's left
Finding places that fit us best

Alone yet surrounded
Making sense of what's said
Meshing bodies in any bed
Opened mind easy head

Give me your lips
Your tenderness
Let me breathe
Your essence in

Curves and flesh
Body gives what's next
Blissful
Happiness

Anticipate
Wonderment
Open ended
Future tense

Welling up like tidal Thor
Tears are speaking so much more
Beyond the ability of lover's score
Letting go of challenges from before

Tip toe to show
Wanting to go
Feeling so deep
Wanting to please

Smiles streak across my eyes
Like golden rays split the sky
Warm my cheeks with kissing lips
Distance bypassed with moments like this

Two places, two tongues
Languages for fun
Outside myself outside you
We find outside with so much to do

Lover, like the petals found on creek side roads
I find like places in my heart that feel like home
Adventures of the body, the earth, the soul
Dancing in between the heart and all that is known

Dusting off faces of facets, we find more happiness
I look to the south, along the sea to where you are
Sing to me in your secret sounds, I'll keep my ear to the ground
Playtime in gardens, rivers and creeks, come out to find me now

Taste me like two buds of lavender
Steeping in your morning coffee
Feel my temperature increase as your eyes close
Roll me around your mouth

Let the energies of our entanglement flow
Thru the soft dimples of your neck that call to my lips
Take me into you as you breathe
Lead me to your damp places and let my essence be buried deep

Remind me, I am of the earth, the land and sky
When we travel our bodies intertwined
Open the heavens, our minds inside
Return to rhythms long since lost
Opening the home to feelings of trust

We are there in the quiet place
Here in our bodies and there in our minds
Beyond our abilities and above our lives
Sitting in this moment and moving thru time

Letting the doors open to what's unknown
The intentions to find something new
So fun, to see it built with interest and intention
No longer needing second or third chances

A thousand dreams that brought me to you
Dreams of wonder, of lust, of complete surrender
I melt within, these silly paper walls
They've been up for who-knows-how-long

With timid touches to shake my core
I let go again, to feel once more
The types of feelings that're truly there
The tears flow, the body knows

Decomposing ideas for fertile flowers
Buds and seeds, for your sweet showers
Beings of love, affection, patience and trust
Setting boundaries before, this wasn't luck

Wake up with me and share this, our silence
Connect deeper, sweetness, our bodies like this
Wrapped and wiggled, naked and pure
Refocus this purpose, to be understood

Consume the concentrate, smoked and seared flesh
Giving up antiquated thoughts, we deepen
Again we look for earthy trust, we're not giving up
Close your eyes, we are inside, this again, we try

Moments make memories
Trust takes time
Lovers like lessons
Risk radiates resilience
Connection counters caution

Kisses keep kindness

Allowing asking aching

Treasured tickles taken

Relishing remembered risks

Intelligent ingrained ingredients

Nightly naughtiness now

Another awesomeness awaits

How lovely, come hither sweet honey bee
Come and rest while you feed from me
My sweet scents, hidden nectar, you'll find no flowers

Neck to neck and eye to eye
I find some buttons that seem to hide
A little flesh to capture my pollen
Let's get together so you can dive in

Such a wonderful image
I love moments like this
Where you feel safe
I find more ways

Celebrating connection
Just 6 more days

Good morning sweet flower
Whose petals have yet to unfurl

Good morning beautiful melody
Whose sound has hit my ears

Good morning loving mother
Whose children have yet to awake

Good morning keeper of kind eyes
Whose vision has yet to see the world

Good morning seeking embrace
Whose arms have yet to wrap around me

Good morning warm meal
Whose nourishment has yet to be devoured

Good morning strong warrior
Whose strengths have yet to be used today

I miss you like mornings parting with the setting moon
I miss you like sand longing for the laughter of children
I miss you like fog that kisses the calm waters of a lake
I miss you like leaves departing slowly from their branches

I miss you as much as coffee beans waiting for hot water
I miss you as much as a swing desires movement
I miss you as much as a piano seeks to sing
I miss you as much as a pan wants a flame

I do not love you
Yet, adore how your skin feels like something I've always
known
Your lips, warm me like sunshine growing the world
Your fingertips inform me of all the places you've been

I do not love you
Yet, count the hours and minutes left until we embrace again
Our pressure together, envelopes, quieting the world
Shared space, soft circle, our breaths and beats become one

I do not love you
Yet, am holding back biblical waters of emotion
Seeping in from every action, intensity, like spouting horns,
mist us
We are in flow, deep waters welling up for a chance in the sun

I do not love you
Yet, imagine myself like dust, duff, flowers and fluff
Caught up in your wings and winds spiraling outward and
inward
We travel together, I give up, let go, it's time, you know

Distance brings a test of strength
Pulling strings to test their length
Touching them where the heart connects
Counting them until there's no distance left

Vibrations felt in the time between
Threads spun out, but never seen
Connections with our hearts and heads
This is how we build our web

Like me, a man one tear left to meet the land
Comprised of thoughts and directions, feels lost
A single tear, departing, speaks so much
A single man, departed, to get in touch

Where am I, with you, feels discovered
Open eyes, we two, confirm connection
Sound and space, energy everyone makes
I stand surrounded, looking for you in this place

I look back, in body, memories of time
Shattered and scattered these pieces of mine
Your hands sliding, finding in darkness, just fine
Pieces whose meaning gets reassigned

Distances expanded while our base grows
Something the silence inherently knows
Restoration in effect, there's but one action left
Go, be, feel and do, united since the day we met

My little kitten was found on a lake
Clutching some lilies to stay in place
Golden from her curls to her bright kind smile
She said, I'm holding these in place to stay awhile

Concert on the water, to let the sound in
Echoing off the mountains, catching trees living
Treats and drinks to follow the flow
So many others floating here also know

Saturated with sunlight and small little waves
Ebbs and flows, with you I wanna stay
Warm as the sunshine, it's only time
Holding us in place, saying you're mine

Dappled and reflected, the sunlight shines
Focused and reflecting, it's the sound that finds
In and thru the connection, feelings of us two
It's an adventure, seeking with trust is what we do

First touches of fall, upon the foliage
Like the fingertips of trees
Its color connects to the sugar it needs
Shows what season's next

Along the roads and paths we take
A river runs, it knows it's safe
Such golden light dapples all over the ground
Such golden light dapples you and I now

Sunlight, sometimes blinding
Sometimes a river winding
With stops and rests
We go and go until there's nothing left

Surrounded by moving humanity
Yet, we seek times where it is just you and me

Pulling pictures from your paintings
Placing them in our vision, we see
Such sweet connections, abilities
Perfection and I'm honored it's me

I enjoy my morning workouts
Repeating the little things you say
When you touch me
How you like this part or that

How you enjoy receiving me
In my total strength
Your expressions of safety and size
Bring me a joy and satisfaction

You see and know all this
As you are all this
You are more than this
Inspiration, kitten

I work my body as my mind
I work my mind as my body
As a means for myself
Also for your entanglement

Like newly sprouted tips of evergreen
Small round birds that jump instead of fly
Crows darting and dashing throughout the skies
You, little kitten, have captured my mind

When walking thru spaces filled with energies
Scented breezes, strong gusts or chilly air
On beach time or our bodies bare
You, little kitten, remind me to reflect

Beautiful scenes, simple beauty
Endearing love, fully lovely
Patient acceptance, quiet stillness
Historical awareness, present tense

Swelling with seasons all felt in one day
My seeds ripening after a full flowering
Time you choose to life alongside
Rhythms and flows, our bodies know why

Like leaves growing strength in their stems for a wind they
haven't felt
Like waves holding and building energy for a shore they haven't
crashed
You are the growth of life to my breezes of love
I am the crashing of water unto your moving sandy shores

Like a rainbow radiant in the sky intermixed with the mist,
looking to double its beauty
Like colors finessing themselves thoughtfully in the sky, our
eyes seek understanding
I am the droplets that suspend and showcase your ability to
connect
You are the fingertips dabbing my colors for all to see

You and I mixed up and mixed together
You are as I am you

Connectedness corrected
Stabilizing strengths
Exposing love
Vulnerable
Cautious
Present
Freely
True
You
Me

Listening to pillowed heartbeats
Happy fresh feet
On recently rained streets

Where humor finds coffee on the side
Of history's river
Where a drawbridge is timed

I've always wanted to run in the dark
Full on, as fast as I can, without stopping
When the moon is resting and can't see the stars
An aerial down blanket, floating and nesting

Completely safe and full freedom
It's terrifying and hasn't been done
There's too many trips, trees and buildings
It'll never be safe enough for me

Then we kissed
Anointed with ocean mist
Golden light
It changed my mind

Vision is different
Ability is free
Obstacles dissolve
Now that you're around

Life is open, able and free
Floating by or thru, we get to choose
It's so simple, we simply do
Quietly, it's just us two

Sooo, as I learn to float above and thru
I'm lovingly, looking to you
To remind me, that stumbles and trips
Are quite normal for something like this

See me as I'm able
Hug me into my past
Love me into our future
Kiss me for this moment, at last

Moving mountains never knew the size
Making love is making time
Don't have a second chance
Just living a manifested life

Going in to give it strength
No longer bonded to a maze
Get in closer, here's my face
Connected, no matter the place

You let me open up as a true man
More than twice as much as I had
Fully feeling my power and it's no big deal
Strong in yourself, you too are being real

Quiet steps leading into the woods
Listening to the layers as best we could
Gentle reflection, deep inhalations
We look around, having childish fun

But then, our bodies instinctively reach
Having kept the lessons this is where we meet
You said you knew what all I contained
Life stories and life in drawers, this is how I'm made

Are we leaning in, are we balanced or tilting

Seems we've discovered the finish line, looks like we win

It doesn't go unnoticed how sunshine finds your face
From little slivers of mornings streaked across your cheeks
To golden immersions when the sun kisses the horizon

It doesn't go unnoticed how the night sky plays with you
From shooting stars streaking below the milky way
To light of Arcturus that takes parts of you back home

You are beauty in motion

I love you at the crossroads of warm blankets and a cool breeze
I love you like the mornings where slowness is felt and seen
I love you while the birds stretch and preen their wings
I love you as the sunlight brings us brand new colored beauty

I love you from the places where my bones and muscles meet
I love you like the textured and measured bites of food we eat
I love you as hot as the sweetened coffees we drink
I love you softly like a fuzzy blanket as you nuzzle into me

I love you like the butterflies that dance from your eyes
I love you quietly, like coastal forest stillness frozen in time
I love you passionately like classical notes all intertwined
I love you in all the healthy ways we can say, you're mine

Good morning sweet holder of protected space
My night was held by your distant embrace
I wrapped myself in cocoon-like nest
Woke up from a safe night's rest

No alarm needed to wake today
Dreams were wild, that much I'll say
From strangers meeting
To feelings of leaving

I forgot what it's like to start with a smile
Getting right up, it lasts for a while
Kitties are happy and very chirpy
Loving moments like this, feeling quite worthy

You are the pink beneath my morning clouds
Like your colors, to taste, I know how
I call them, simply, into my mouth
Consumed for knowledge, devoured

Miracle of maths
Equations like that
Experiences yet had
Eyes naughty, be bad

Take my weathered feet to the woods for play
Accept these handsome hands to place on your face
Bloom your sweetened skin for my nose to trace
Synchronicities, energies confirming embrace

Close your eyes for a special place for me
Tickles dance under and thru your skin, I see
I know distance in a thought, you're in my head
I know the distance of a heart, take hold these threads

Crash into me in all your ways, let me feel your waves
Wash over to soak into me, minerally
I see your sweet strength, I feel your depths
I stand on the shore, naked, there's nothing left

A river canyon to feel the depths
Overhead sun can't take a rest
Exposed faces make the cliffs
In your cool waters I want to sit

Emotional I go, each and every day
I flurry for moments, I am this way
Your flow anchors me, my safest place

Rivers love cliffs
It is where canyons exist
No fears persist
With connection like this

With mere hours for mere flesh
Minutes to count to see what's left
Our spaces are tidy, there's no mess
We'll cuddle, kiss and connect

Heavy weather with intense energy
Heavy feelings connect you and me
Ocean in an uproar, the mighty sea
Leaves are falling, slippery streets

Where we travel to verify our love
It's in the magic of forest cuts
The ways you came before the missed rain
How we split the sky, magic you'd say

We came back thru an illumination
A golden matrix, a composition
We travel thru to this life we exist
More than heaven we persist

I want to enter you like the morning sun
Where it starts in the dark, fully enveloped dotted with stars
Twilight lifts where a spectrum of greys exist
Then a peek of what may be, a color here, what do we see

Brighten our day, gradually it's made, as a few colors slide
Powder us with soft touch clouds, a few streaks across the sky
Eager to be a witness to the pink accents, parts of our soul
Beaming gold to power it all, just before the sun is exposed

You hold me and I hold you, wrapped together, sunlight knows
Hearts open in clouds like hearts open to the world
Reflections in nature, overwhelming joy we witness
Fully feel this moment, intertwined no mistakes

Let us both be waves
In oceans and in lakes
Frigid or in heat
Be next to me

Let our energies
Be our wakes
Sandy shores
Where we lay

Moody and gorgeous
We take the world with us
Made of salt or fresh
We take the breath

Curl and lift
Merge and split
Slide and rip
Flat and spindrift

Blend us true, morning pink and sky blue
We stretch for the gold like mountains do
Held in between but feeling my seams
About to burst, so much in this world

I ache for more yet hardly control
Full vision but wanting more
Been passing thru, loves at the door
Exposed and expanded, I'm yours mi amor

With schools of thought and lessons taught
I wake on mornings where our touch is not
Longing, waiting, spare parts of me are lost
Entered into a web of love, I'm caught

Along the ways I have seen a few built
Some hastily made and some with skill
Your technique is what I desire most
This is what I'd like you to know

Family recipes old and new
Well traveled maps lead me to you
Mistakes in the moment changed the course
Growth from the memories so now I'm yours

Spinning inside and flicking off doubt
Trusting and loving, so this is how
Comforting calmness the healthy routine
Proud of myself, happy you're with me

Shaking my head to loosen it up
Knocking off things to use for growing stuff
Like patience, connections and our love
Happiness, memories and our trust

There you are, my morning love, mixed with me, my dear
Doesn't matter the distance, your hands are still here
Slowly, gliding, finding all their favorite places, as they please
I wake happy, that soon, I will no longer use memories

Your loving power is here now
Droplets of you bouncing round
Your breaths find me with the wind
As soon as I wake I take them in

Whole face smiles, eyes and teeth
Are just the beginning of what you do to me
My mind is alive, the feeling of safety
Hours until it's in whispers we speak

Slowed down sunset where the colors breathe
Living longer on our love, the merging energies
So simple, music needs connectings
The minutes slowing us into the hourly

Collecting petals, feathers and grains of sand
Complementary items make memories last
Threaded thru the fibers of earth
Stars connected, magic midlife rebirth

Rippled like water, enjoying the sand
Stubborn yet trying, receiving as a man
Stern skin and soft lips grip my attention
Arousal needs no mention

Numbers of mine, you sure do have
Belief in the action, makes me glad
Look below the water line
See the grains, drifting by

Alone in the sun, heat we withstand
Water slides in meeting the land
Divine energies exchange, balanced
Encounterers given this chance

Spent, exhausted and depleted
I felt and feel you still love me
I give and gave until I found no other way
Content to not continue, connected we lay

I used it all, more than the best
Action until there's nothing left
Deep smiles for this layer of rest
Natural beauty in all my mess

Blown up from the south, love fueled by your mouth
The wind rips into my body, releasing doubt
I hear earth songs, echoes and spells
Bearing witness to nourishing ocean swells

Distracted, stay focused
It's in us, let's do this
A few weeks away
From the yes you'll say

Rest within my fortified walls, safe and warm
I'll be your golden lighthouse against any storm
Restore your strengths as your eyes slowly close
Climb up and let it all go as only your body knows

Once inside, protected and caressed
Healing continues to see what's next
With powers more than I can understand
I stand lovingly before you a healing man

Distance between
Us this evening
Multiplies feelings
In these beings

Yuck taste
Sour mouth
Cloudy mind
Blow it out

Hot shower
No rest this hour
Night scene
Cleansing breeze

Honest words
Heart hurts
Stay connected
Sounds projected

Eyes release
Tears and cries
Mind finds
Not left behind

Buffalo my big ol head
Hours until I'm safe in your bed
Digital and distance isn't the same
Still grateful for these modern ways

Baaaaabe, my heart is being tested
You are literally manifested
Still feeling scared with some of these steps
Still moving forward until there's no distance left

Thank you for pins and pictures you've placed
My heart, my walls, the inner feelings, safe
You've taken looks around, stayed for a while
You stop and let me sink in, still all smiles

A perfect wave, with a perfect curl
A perfect color, with a perfect swirl
A perfect crash, with a perfect rip
A perfect wind, with a perfect mist

A wave like your arms, strong and curvy
A color like your hair, sunkissed and curly
A crash like your distance, time is ripped
A wind like your kisses, deeply missed

Filling up waves on an autumn afternoon
Folding in for beauty, the ocean, she chooses
Undaunted in a line, she steadily marches towards me
Tirelessly she defies gravity so beautifully

She shows me how to love with power
Less of a man I'd be without her
She shows me where beauty is from
Realizing her abilities and love, I've come

Walking up and into your arms, home once again
Soft touches begin, the connections strengthen
How much time it's been, flows with rivers, blows with winds
Happiness, the feelings of knowing, our hearts sing

Mornings of lavender skies, subtle streaks of rose pink
Merging of our energies, mornings of combined routines
One more moment, three more kisses, sacred blessings
Partnership in motion, solid commitment, healthy trusting

Love, I live to honor your existence
To anchor myself, like the land
I'm open and fertile, ready for growth
Batter and bathe me with your weather

I live with your rains and winds
Your deepest feelings within
You rest upon my heaviness
Knowing, solidly, he can take this

Together we change and create
We dissolve, mix and stay up late
With rest and rays we rejuvenate
Little pieces we give and take

Love, when seconds feel like days
When distance complicates
As tears fall and feelings take place
Recall our bodies, loving memories made

Your sights, in their intense and natural beauty
Arrest me, to admire, mind shifts and you move me
There is submersion and steeping
Whole energy magnetism, no desire of leaving

Pour into mouth, with sacred actions
Divinity in the method, appreciation that lasts
Sit for a while, melt away from masks
Reach the peaks, finishing with laughs

Alone and on the lookout for energy reception
I wondered around appreciating nature's perfection
Am I coming in clear or did distraction warp my waves
I've been practicing my manners, wild and behaved

Like a bear in the woods nested under sitka roots
I crave your protection, earthy, whole and smooth
So carefully wrapped, earthy seasons pass
I've made myself a home, having found my other half

We dance around moons, planets and stars
Molded of stardust, hours aren't far
Feelings within us, that's where this starts
Now it's clearing up, why those endings were hard

Softness now has never been so felt
Mesmerizing eye gazes, might be a spell
Assurance of connection, overflowing wells
Sweetly secure, discarding cards dealt

Alone and on the lookout for energy reception
I wondered around appreciating nature's perfection

Permissions to lift you with all your strengths
No matter the weight

As the wind I carry you over mountains
Above the bays

We've mixed with double rainbows
Feathers and rain

Decades of dreaming condense into
Hours and days

Through the depths and debris
There you are with me
Full of love, swimming

Through a life you would go
There, your body knows
With one, it's so cold

Buoyant still so deep
You're there with me
Generating heat

Which parts of me are the curtain of clouds
Framing your parts in the colors setting now
Colors and clouds nighting with the setting sun
It's at night, naturally, when we blend into one

Naked in our nature
Exposed before her
We're observed
Dually pleasured

Unpredicted
Less restricted
We persisted
Que buena vista

A lesson from the wind
Not every feather flies in the end
A few are fluffing up in the beginning
Some drift into a hat's brim

We're full of features
Some for focus
A few for pleasure
Even deeper, designed for love

Obstacles and observations
Finding the places we stretch from
Vibrations thru eyesight
Love softens our mind

Speechless and speedy
My mind goes quickly
Handsy and seeking
My body's craving

Misaligned times
Trauma lies
Memories hide
Internal pride

Senses overloaded need a shift
Let the softness exist, embrace and sit
What's the process, what pieces did I miss
Holy wonders, you have me, wholly like this

Allowed to be at this precision
The exact millisecond of decision
My fears holding for protections
My loves pulling for progression

You've had the lessons
Years of sessions
Exactly the intention
Authenticity represented

You have the outs
I've said them twice now
One more disclosure
Keep my composure

Physically responsive
Audibly exhausted
Cellularly pleasured
Lovingly tethered

You see my speed
I see your ease
I feel your need
You fill my scene

Dancing round the plates
Plants into food we make
Smiles and joy on our face
Imbibing in our faves

When the air holds our bodies
Allows for flows we have always known
No longer pressured by expectations
Our experiences become more than us

Moving past the pains
Of traumatic yesterdays
Mind or body, who behaves
Attempting to articulate

Mornings made into moments
Subtle sacredicity and we go with
Open ourselves for divine diving
The oldest we've been, perfect timing

First rays skipping down the side of your hill
Where foxes and deer blow kisses, natural thrill
The future is there, glowing and growing
Your mind is focused, active and knowing

Catching the rays, kisses and growth
Days and times to be slow
We have moments like this
Already better, joyous

Reflect from me and I see you
Ocean is calm, shades of blue
Ripples of sand, truest beauty
Laughing or playing together we're pleased

Flatten and reflect
Clouds and ocean don't mix
They dance with sun
Since before we've begun

How many sunsets need to be seen
To distinguish between know and believe
Being ready and knowing right away
So many reasons, I'm here to say

The lights in your eyes that beam true love
A believer of goodness you've been sent from above

The many ways we connect, loving literature and art
So many threads when we spool out our hearts

The sharing of history from our previous lives
A mutual understanding, an omission of whys

The loving of nature, appreciation of the outdoors
Divine acceptance and encouragement, I'm yours

How many stars need to shine
To enhance "I'm yours and you're mine"
Being rested and patient, sound the way
Brought us to the moment, our today

When memories and masks overwhelm my space
I seek connections of ours, your loving face
Save me from floating away inside
Keep me from running and trying to hide

I trust in the love as you have presented
I hold onto the connections that you have given
My grip is strong to match fear and love
At times, I wish we were just one

To use and remember your powerful traits
Allows me to grow from remembering your strengths
Worries with warrior, it's all of me
Holding me close, it's all I need

One silver strand stretched between my hands
A lifetime of growth, a long hair for a man
It changes at the end, a bit of youthful brown
A window of my life, yet I'm holding it now

So we share in our age a transition of sorts
A hunger for life still seeking more
We travel and witness nature at her best
We love and we give until there's nothing left

As a man in this stage it's important to say
I'm lucky, I'm grateful to be loved in your way
I feel seen, I feel held, I feel accepted by you
I'm seen, I'm held, full of love, it's true

Mornin, noon and moments at night
You travel in my body, heart and mind
Taking little pieces to inspect and dust
A lover like this who loves just because

I feel all the warmth, golden steps left
Clearing and cleaning, this isn't a mess
You steep, you see so many parts of me
I stand prouder, in knowing, you believe

To have done some work with parts of self
Weeding and tilling, planting on earth I've knelt
Praying and playing into a lovable man
Palms up, heart open, it's you who understands

Perfection, best used for right where you're at
Love for each other, acceptance makes it last
Safe for a cuddle, cuss and or a fuss
Safe for a lifetime when built with trust

Passing between qualities
Naming the books in my libraries
Presenting myself to be seen
Holding forgiveness for the past me

Part in the moment, part make believe
Grown in the middle of society
Depends each case: fem or masculinity
Standing balanced, I'm called Riley

So as the name is placed
From the middle life is traced
Called since birth, that's my name
Oldest, yet the second, I began that way

With all that weight, history and lore
You've shown up, saying gimme some more
Who's to say what'll be in our store
We've updated threads and strings to loving cords

Ice cubes like wind chimes on a mist and starry night
Four eyes meet in the dark, kisses illuminating with a spark
Our beats and feets slow their pace to match the moon
Hands held for warm connection and our cosmic growth

With increased interactions that leave us mind blown
We breathe out little old voices that whisper
Instead we stand tall, chest to chest in trust
A smile for each other, always in love

Chilly fall winds breeze around in our space
Stepping finely and firmly into the unknown
We've gone to some, others yet to go
There's little left outside but falling in love

Tip toe in the dark I'll take your hand from the start
This is your mirrored river and still woods after all
There's drips and drops from the mist and stars
With a light we won't trip, there's Venus and Mars

Naughty in nature, there's a bench that's wet
In the dark jellies came and then the tide left
Hearken back to secret trails when we just met
Water's presence in, around and thru, we're blessed

Pass the trust to me in the dark
I can see the trail and where we parked
Trust me in, the trails of your dark place
We're meeting in the light, kissing your face

Worthwhile travels let the body go for a bit
Practice patience, nuances not missed
Another night closer to us giving in
Love loving thru moments, with you like this

What began as seeded notes
Writing letters to see what's sown
Planted then to watch them grow
We feel the roots deep below

A simple flower is fine here or there
Gives us pause to stop and stare
A stem sturdy to support the buds
There's nothing like earth's love

We are here to witness
When we choose life like this
It's almost impossible to miss
Many moments to reminisce

A single wave with a curl of beauty and balance
An ocean in the moment, slow mixture; it's flat
Colors of autumn complementing your complexion
An extension of nature's beauty, you're what she's done

The sheer strength you contain
Overtook the struggles, this life you've made
Bringing me on board, crash against my shore
I'll hold you up, love, there's nothing more

Fear of failures based on the past
Who wants to bring memories of how they didn't last
A different time, such ability to mask
We bring it forward, with healing, we laugh

Let me fall to your fertile forest floor
Where my flowers can grow once more
Where breaths are left instead of regret
I'll give fully into whatever we create next

You have my history, my imperfections
I present myself for our love to function
I'll stay quiet during reflection
Looking from the future, we'll say, we chose us

I love you before, during and after feelings of uncertainty
The way you're in here with me stays at an ease
Building into the trust, there's intention plus luck
We've taken this chance to begin a time-lapse

Softness on the surface, solid strength just below
We've allowed the other access to paths to go
With open communication and a loving hand
We take walks into intentional-land

I see asking why, could be disbelief
Balancing the questions of why me
To sit, in trust, love --the feelings--
Go against false dichotomies

Our woody friends show a way
The magic and movement as they sway
They never stop growing as they dance about
Connection underground, their foundation is how

As this man that I inhabit, this body this mind
I seek my own understanding, so many whys
But here before you, I seek connection, unique
Every moment grateful, that you do love me

Before, we --you and me-- had unfortunate events
Beyond our control from unhealthy women and men
Actions we've sworn with our soul won't commit
Bonds never broken with new love like this

A lifetime of smiles and pleasing many others
Issues with our fathers and even our mothers
Attempted corrections with the best of our brains
Beaten and broken, we did the best in our ways

Thousands of hours of not so quiet reflections
Writing and crying and yelling, not distractions
Intention and courage led us on a voyage of health
With help from everyone, love, we wrote our own spells

Magic manifested, when softness and strength meet
Our ideal person, materializing, could it be
Nearly to the time where we make the step
We've chosen to give a try, since the day we met

I have gathered my safety like scattered flowers and fruits
Collected them for years, put up in bunches, for use
Aromas of nervousness and certainty have swirled around
Every day in each moment, feeling more confident now

You see the collection and care, each bundle unique
Time for an inspection, many petals and fruity things
Resting in a nest, assessing the many parts of me
I believe in my care, love and affection, healed abilities

With the love at the forefront thickened with life
I use my experiences and my attempts at being right
To show me the patience and softness to love with strength
Your love and acceptance enhances all me-s you see

I called you here to trace my bark
Feel my growth and learn my scars
See the land surrounding my roots
Come sit awhile while I speak to you

Beauty and I'm the tree
You fascinate me
Delicate skin
Resting strength within

Look up to me to see my crown
Climb upon me, lose the ground
In my earthiness you can trust
Winds will move you and I as one

You're nearly to the top
Keep going don't stop
You'll reach for the stars
At my top you're not far

The apex of joy embraced
Contorted in our face
Standing rooted in place
Slide down when safe

Full and subtle joys of electricity
So much more than you and me
Two bodies travel to the center with speed
Experiencing energies past their forms eagerly

More than human touch we're enhancing our lives
Great golden connections, reciprocal mines
On top of the scars, inside the insecurities
We rest in that center fully embraced

To leave oneself is no easy task
Need to drop all of my masks
To join together is no easy ask
Need reassurance, perhaps a laugh

To leave a community you help build
To join a community over a few hills
To wait for the life when it's in your hands
To show up for a lover as a fullest man

We stripped our egos as well as our clothes
We admitted our faults as we got sand in our toes
We were greeted by others from another place
We held in to our hearts, their beats did we trace

To build up something we can't even see
To trust in something we both believe
To be healed from lives that've been torn
To end up at this Pacific Shore

Magic in the memory
Love transforming
We make the magic
From what others call tragic

In what we contain
Love with the pain
Choosing this way
Come closer, stay

Love like this
Currently exists
Tenderness
Your touch I miss

Making every single day better
Has been in my hopes and plans
In four long months we've arrived
123 days with hearts in our eyes

"Well...here we are," was your first text
"So, here we are," is what I said next
We mentioned our magic and dichotomies
Shared our passions, what made us interesting

You showed up sparkly and unique
So beautiful, brings tears to my cheeks
I mentioned time travel and pairing to thrive
You gravitated to my humor, said who is this guy

Incredible to be here, so many days later
Grateful our past selves did us a favor
In the clouds, thru the waves, the sky above
Deep trust, so crazy, we're nuts, but in love

I'm proof, after ten years of honestly hard work
Five years reflective therapy, acknowledging my worth
Thru pains and attempts, I've collected what's left
For a presentation of self, on this lover's quest

Dozens of books about not giving a fuck and loving self
Somehow they showed me a path, said might as well
Hours and days of crying, I stopped asking why
Instead I began to like myself, less a need to hide

Slowly I trusted that I can call out my abilities
Manifestation, humor, intelligence, wanting to be seen
Diligently with hope I held out for your return
There's little doubt we've met before, beyond earth

In just a few hours, we'll find a pressured embrace
Where I'll squeeze you so tight, you'll kiss my face
You'll stop me where I stand and give me eyes that ask
I'll slide out a smirk and say not yet, with a laugh

Immense joy streaks like the cornflower blue clouds this sunrise
Knowing tonight the sun sets with equal hope in our eyes
In just a few hours I'll travel over rivers, headlands and lakes
To ask you a question, the next step will you take

It's the first time I have felt this honest truth
I'm ready to spend a lifetime with you
Though today marks 4 months of space
In each other's lives, time we did make

You are a goddess, the daughter of the creator
I too am godly, balanced in this world, my heart I'll pour
Lifetimes of textures, lectures and lessons
Partnering in souls, completing this mission

I'll love you past tomorrow
From moments spent yesterday
I'll love you when you're older
Because I too will be that way

I'll love you like the mornings
Each day exquisitely unique
I'll love you like the moonlight
Illuminated we are pleased

I'll love you like the ocean
Held in with land's embrace
I'll love you like the birdsongs
Whose origins have no trace

I'll love you like huckleberries
Hidden along forest paths
I'll love you like 20 sneezes
So much to make you laugh

I'll love you for who you are
In this very moment
I'll love you in more ways
When we go with it

A simple ask
So take a look back
Beginning with breath
I'll share what's left
These are the moments that inside me breathe

Being late for you at a special trail
One that ended with the beginning of this tale
Trustingly you followed me in an unknown place
We sat on ancient flows of lava, hidden away

That one time you took me to a familiar yet foreign land
Encouraged me to abandon what was hang-ups for this man
We stood so quiet, our bodies calling out so loud
Breezes and greetings kept us right in our bodies somehow

Next was a place on the edge of the earth
A spot in the public, high up with the birds
We made a nest made of safety and smiles
We decided right there, let's try for a while

Golden gates of rain, held levitating in place
Secrets in the sand, our footprints leaving a trace
Tears shed from love, offering and fear
Belief in this person, who's standing right here

We didn't change our grip when our fingers were tight
We allowed our bodies to accept this new feeling of right
Chivalry remains in our relationship program
The feeling of being honored, I'll say yes ma'am

To the moments of four months that have yet to be expressed
I'll use my energies in the ways I know best
To honor, to hold, to laugh and for growth
To be patient with myself, you and the lives we love

Our next step, should you choose, may sound silly to ask
But I'd like you to be my partner, may I be your last
Boyfriend for now, since only four months have passed
Knowing full well, in the future, I'll have more to add

Will you be mine, in a more formal way?
A yes is needed for you to say

Afterword: So, did she say yes? She did. It has been an amazing experience thus far. Did I keep writing poems? I sure did. As of now, a second collection of 100 poems has already been written. Again, thank you for the time you have taken to read my poetry. May you be supported in your life by love, by the beauty that surrounds us, and by people who seek to uplift you.

With love,
Riley